This book belongs to

_____

Copyright © 2021 Humor Heals Us. All rights reserved. No part of this book may be reproduced in any form without permission in writing from the publisher. Please send bulk order requests to Humorhealsus@gmail.com Printed and bound in the USA. humorhealsus.com 978-1-63731-115-8

Foxy the Fox's Fourth of July Firework Farts

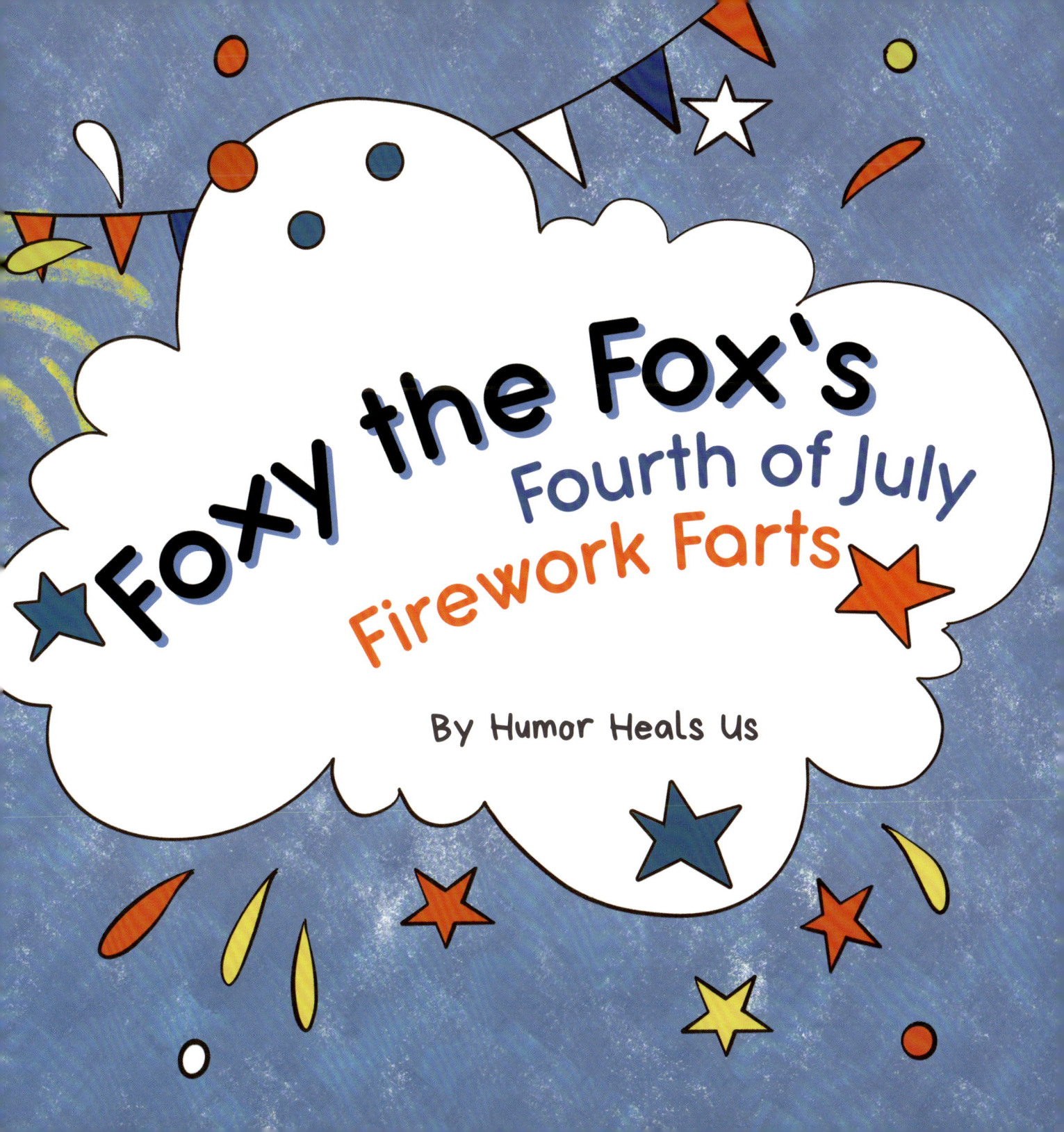

By Humor Heals Us

It's the Fourth of July! That means it's another amazing year of fireworks and farts for me - **Foxy the Farting Fox**.

And if I know anything, I'm an expert at farts on fireworks day! Here are just a few:

GROUND SPINNER

When I start to hear noises in my tummy, I know I'm in for a **ground spinner**. It spins around in my tummy and then it explodes releasing sparks in all directions. Some people call these 'jumping jacks' or "blooming flowers."

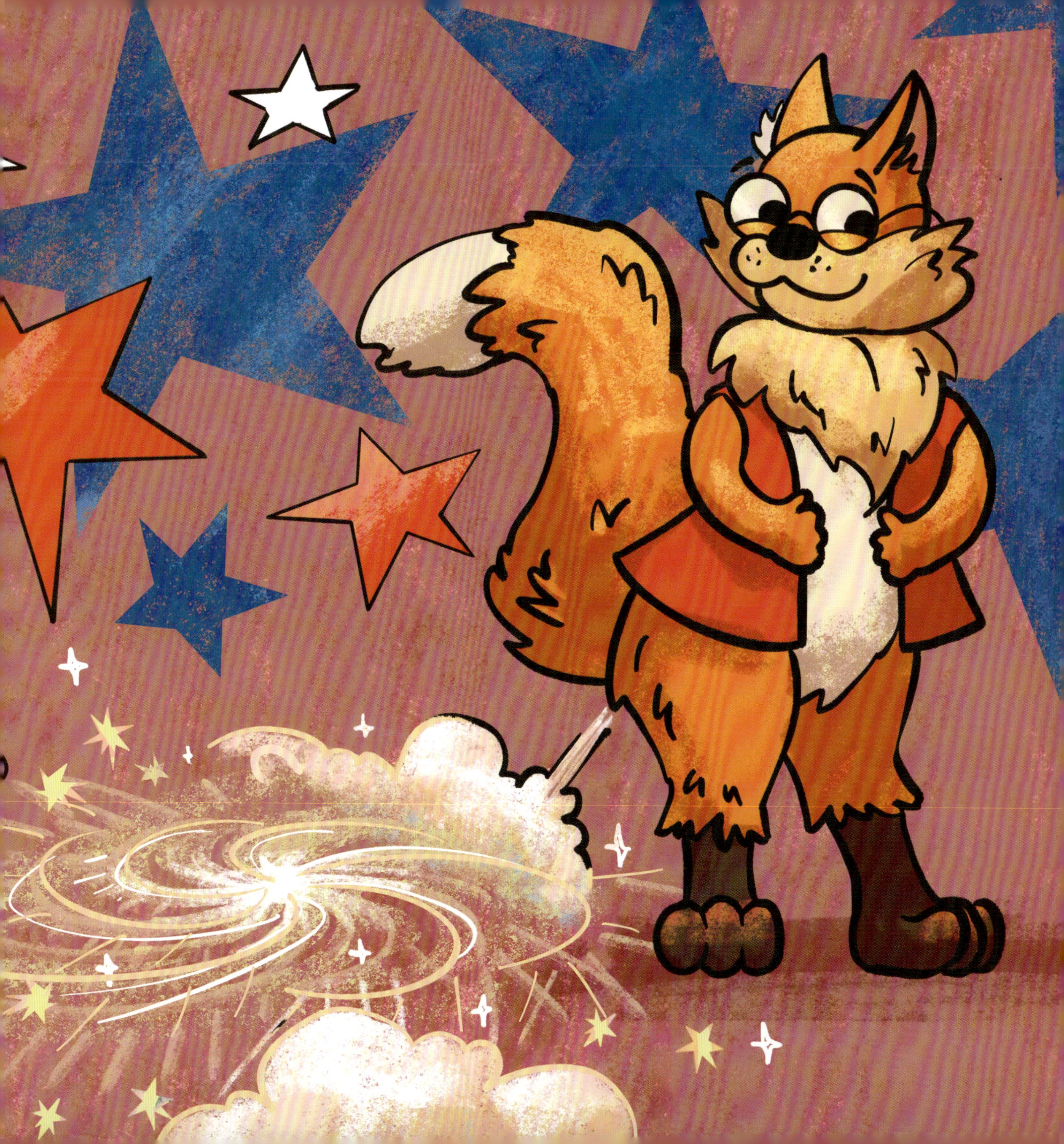

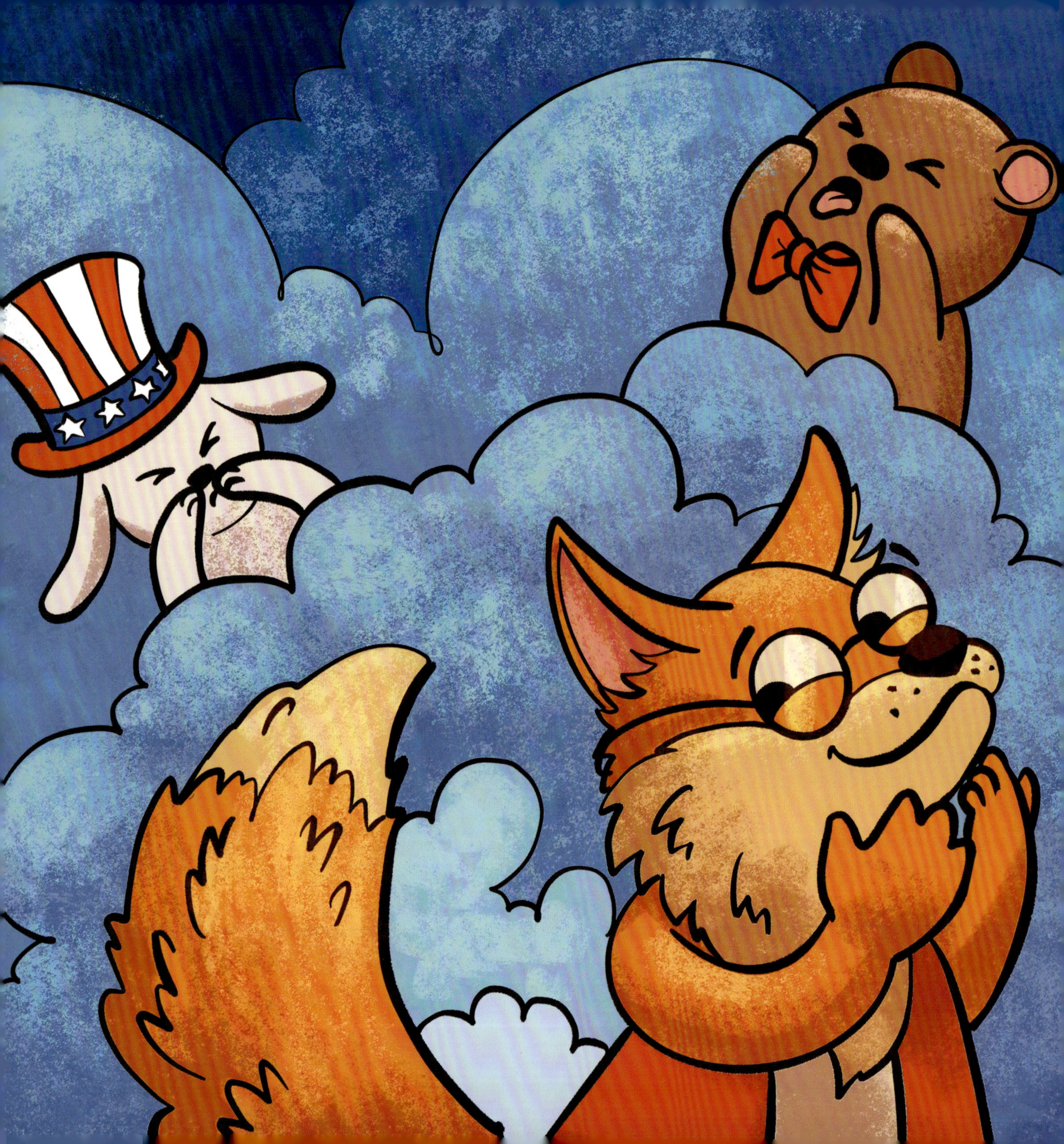

SMOKE BOMBS

Have you ever been in a tight space and let one out and the poor people are prisoners to your **smoke bombs**? Happened to me just this morning.

ARTILLERY SHELLS

My mom likes to make beans for lunch and when she does, sometimes my farts become **artillery shells**, and they shoot up so high into the SKY!

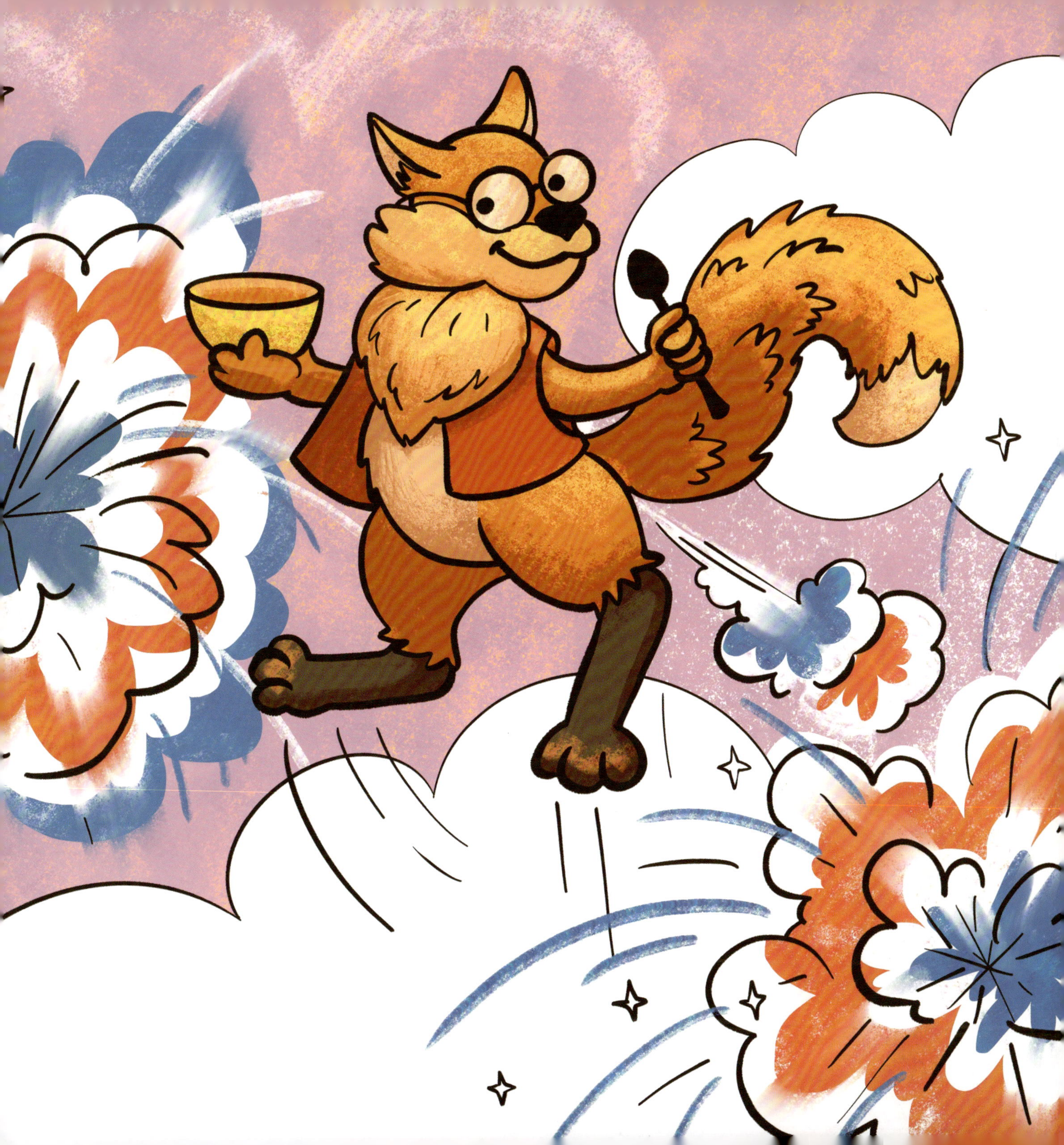

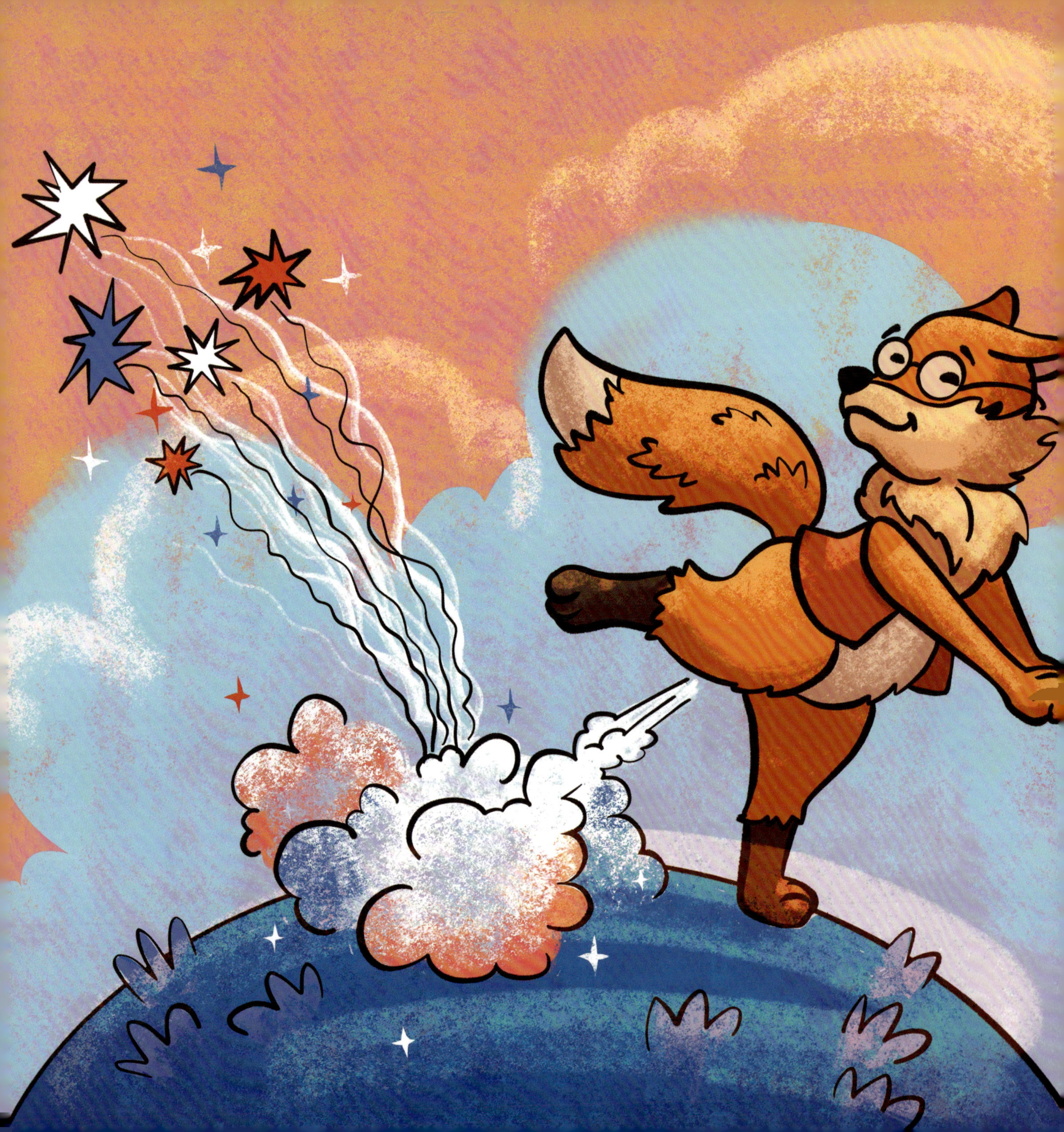

ROMAN CANDLES

Roman Candles will flash, explode, or even crackle for a little bit before they fizzle out completely.

SPARKLING FOUNTAIN

Have you ever farted one and the smell lingers in the air seemingly like forever much like a **sparkling fountain** in the sky? It happens a lot to me and I wish the smell wouldn't linger so long.

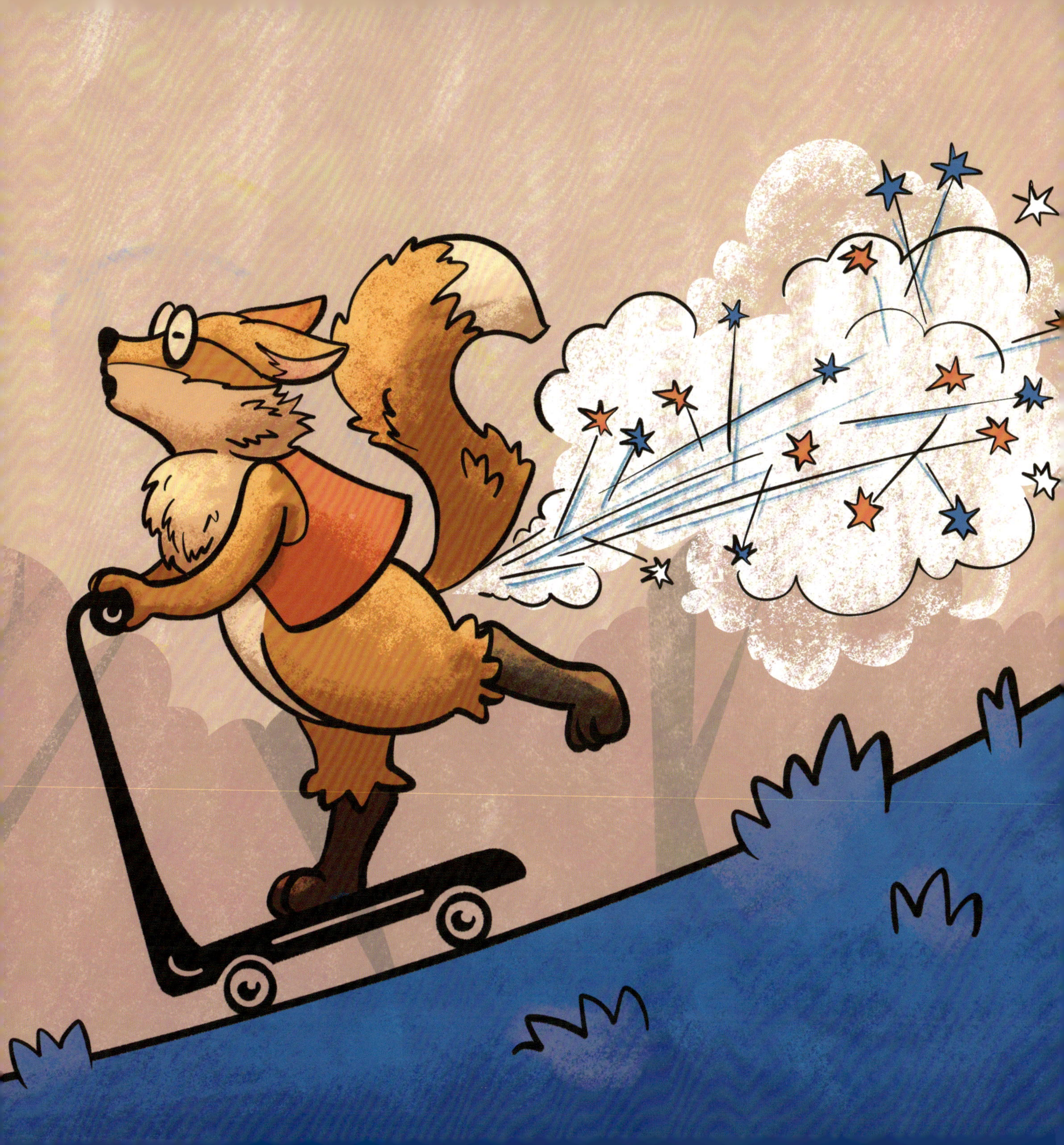

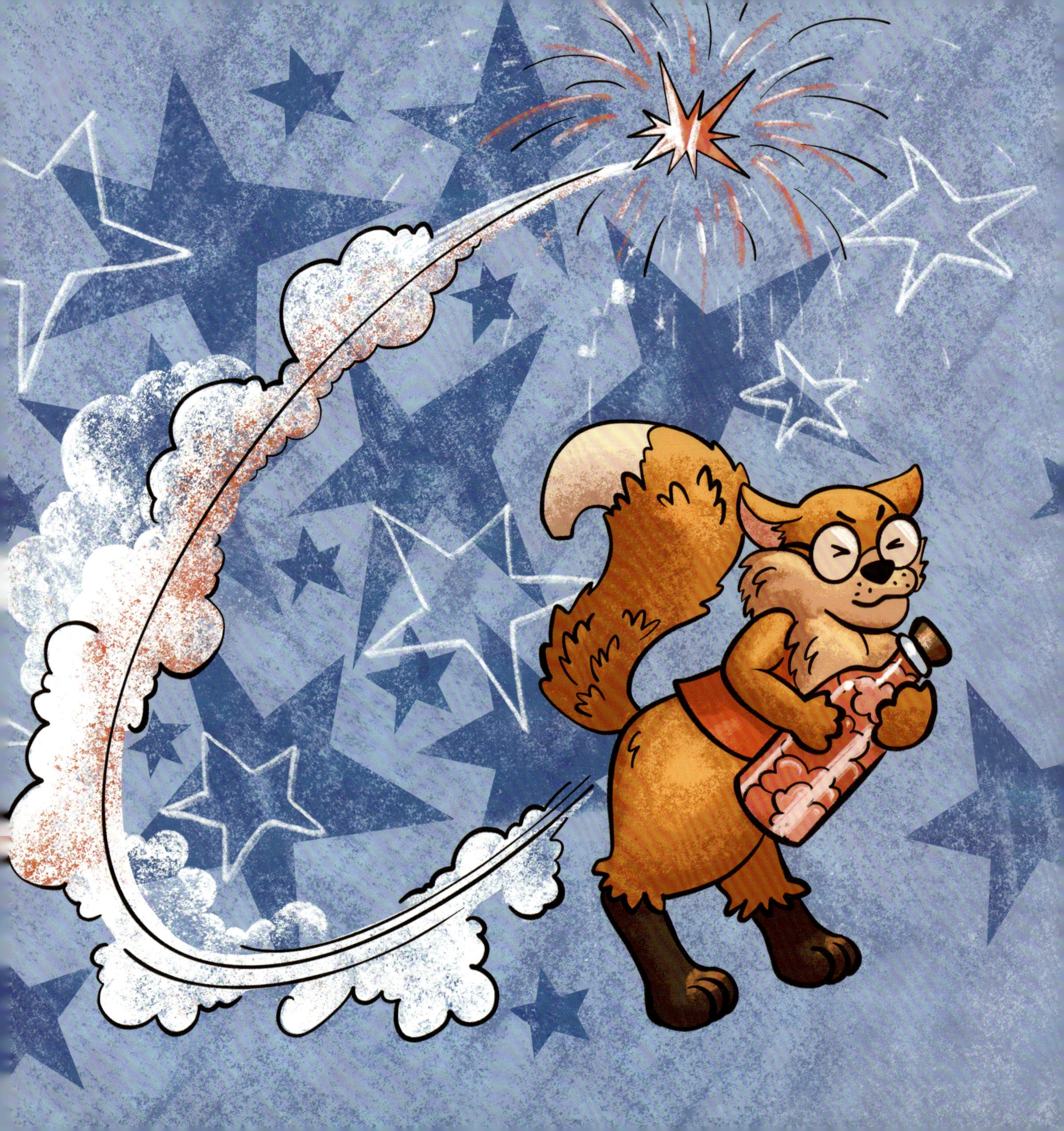

BOTTLE ROCKET

If you've ever heard a whistle and a loud bang, it was probably a **bottle rocket**.

FIREWORK MISSILE

The truth is sometimes the gas inside me gets outrageous and when I finally release it, I shoot off like a **firework missile**!

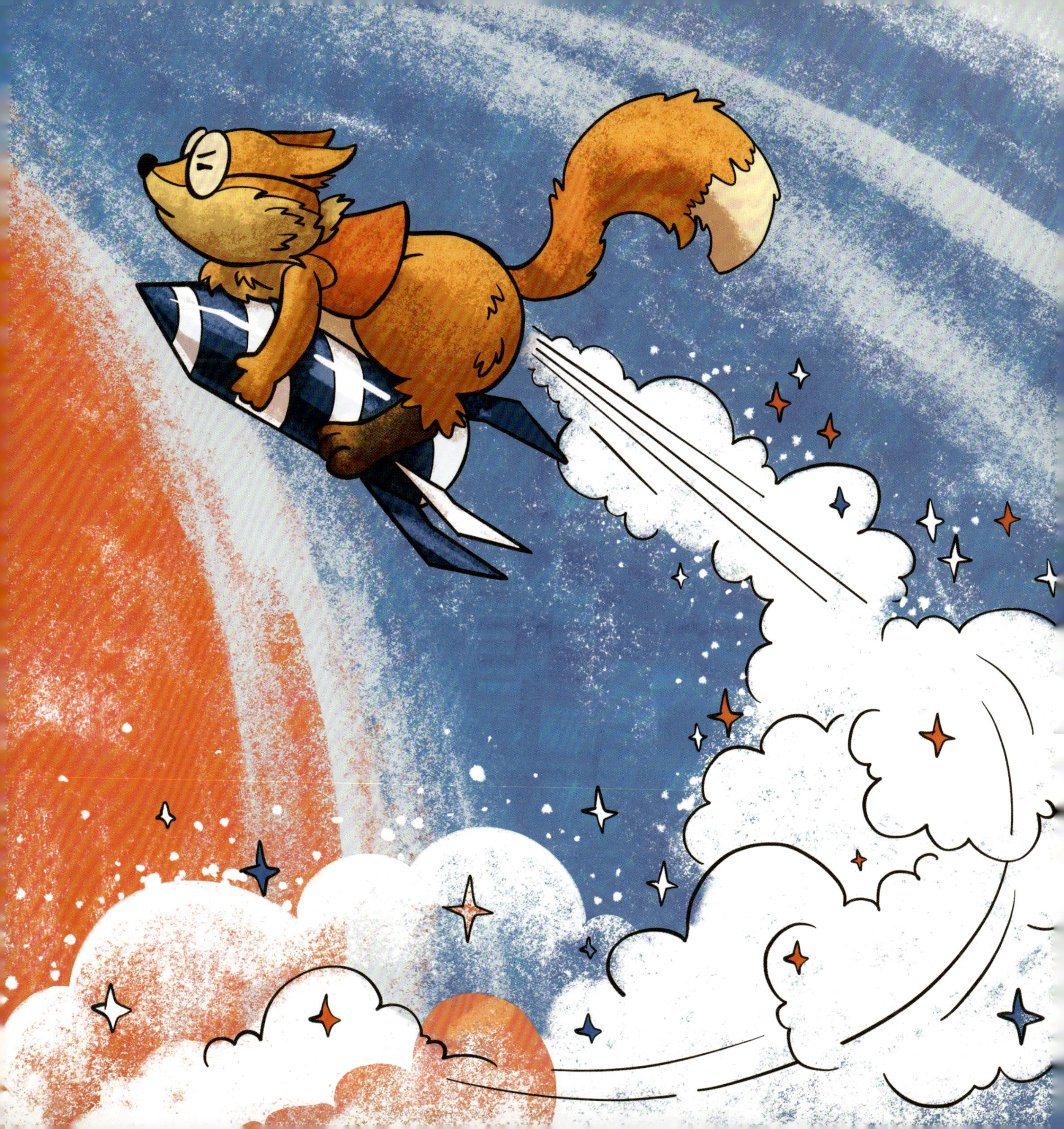

POP!

POPPERS

The most common and normal fart of all is a **popper**. It just POPS out especially when you pull a string.

SPARKLERS

Sparklers are more gentle than some other firework farts but still very noticeable.

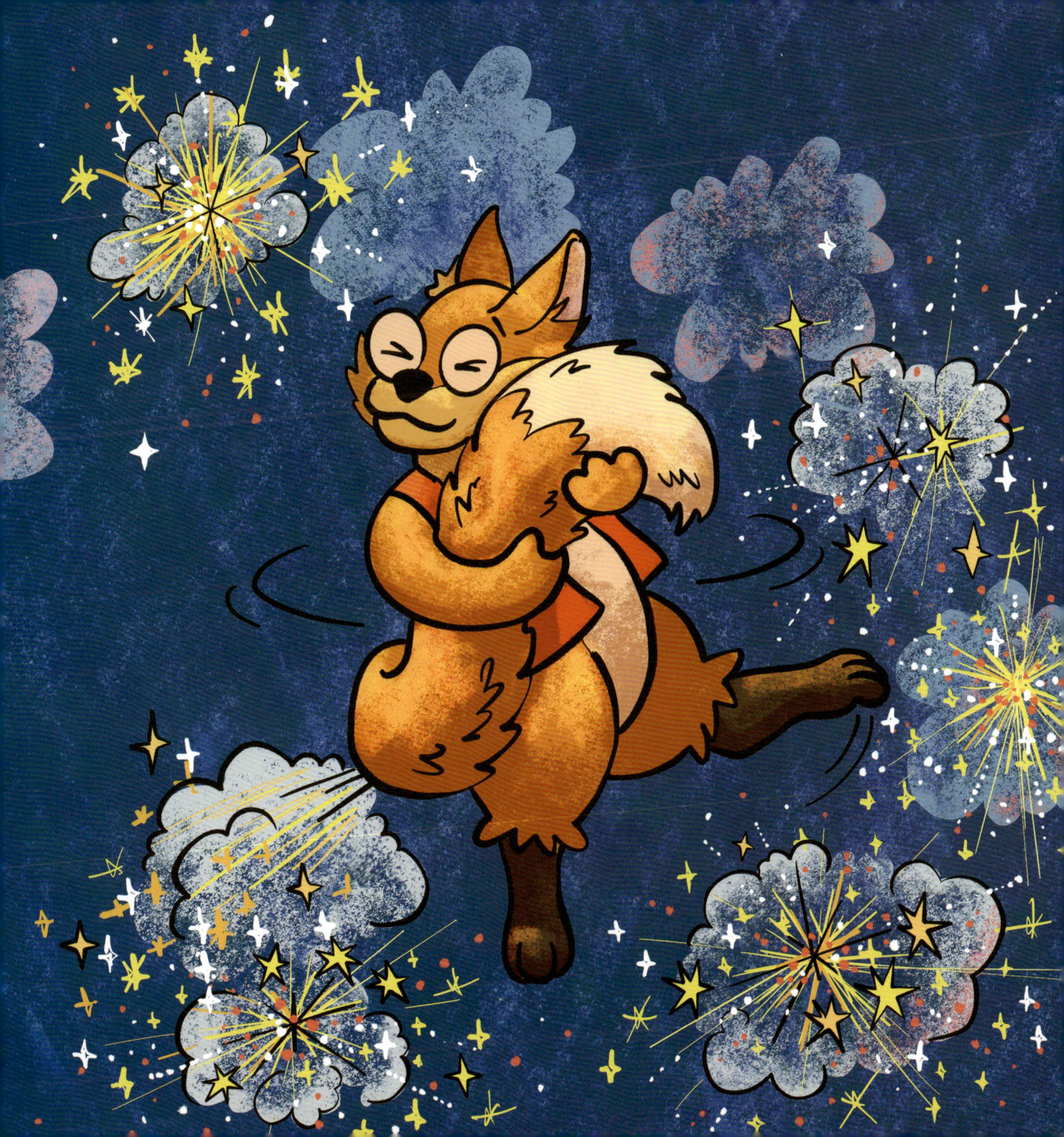

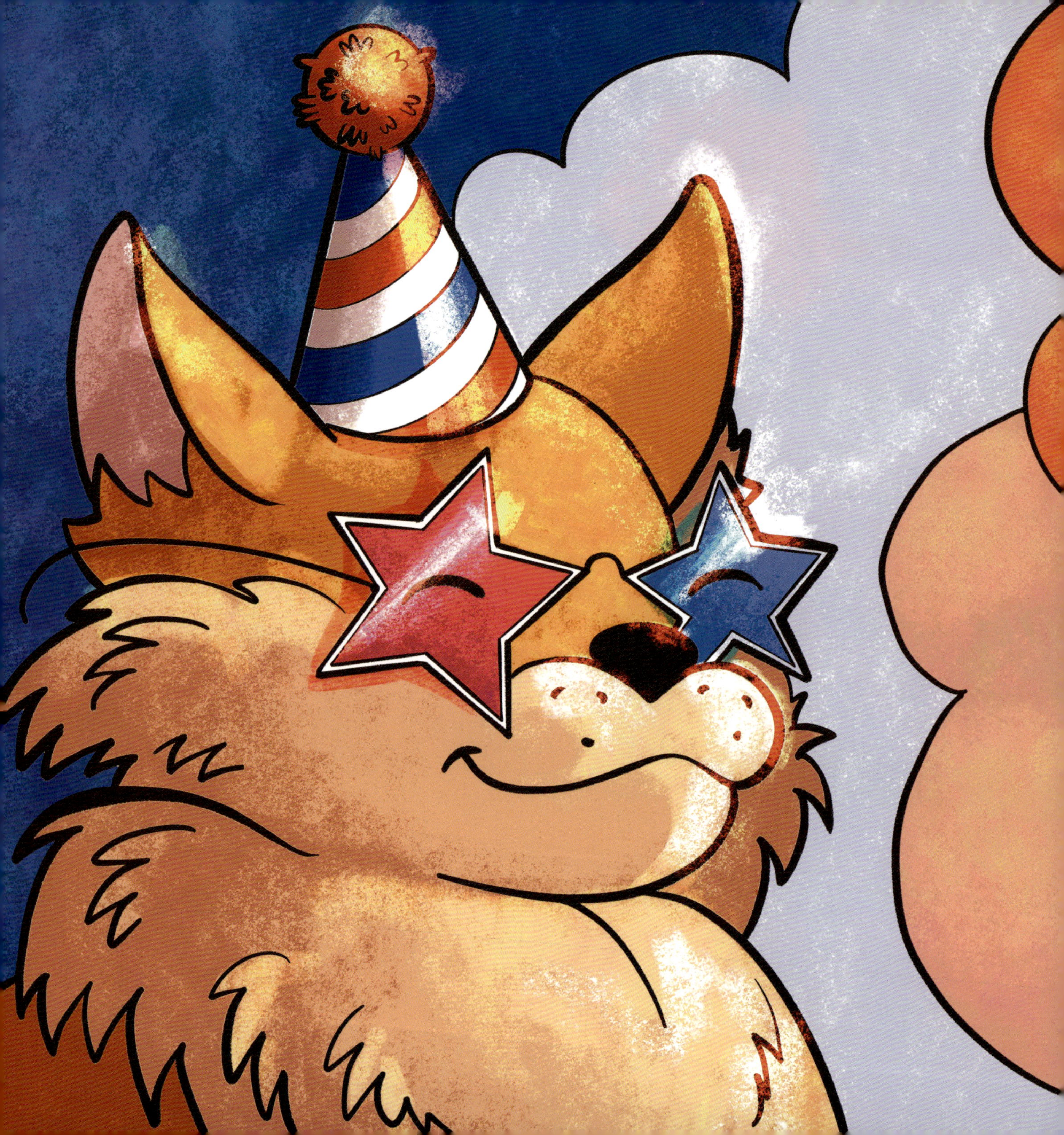

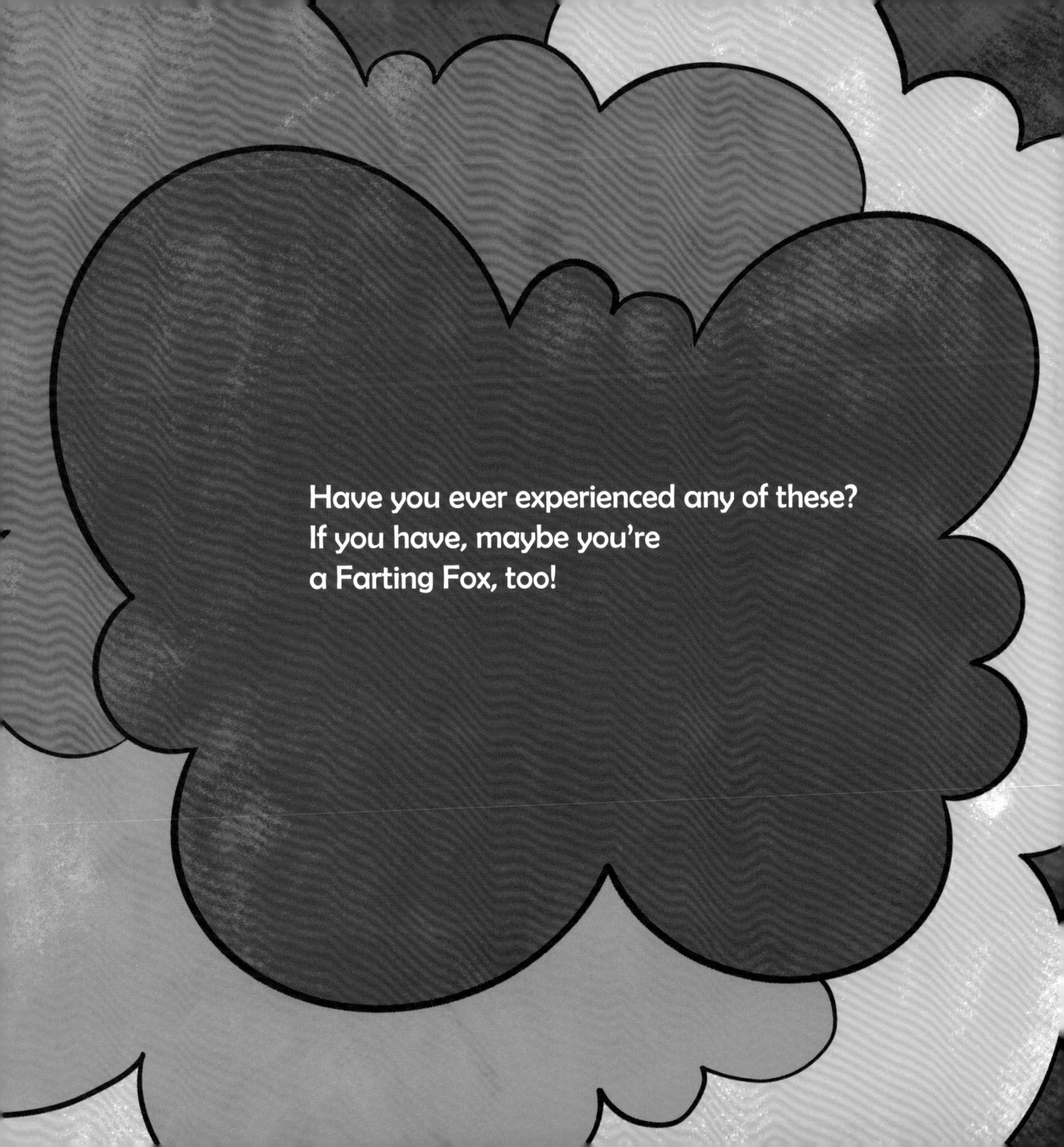

Have you ever experienced any of these?
If you have, maybe you're
a Farting Fox, too!

4th of July

Farting on Fourth of July is normal.
If you don't believe me,
just refer to our next book...
World's Best ~~Farter~~ Father.

Follow us on FB and IG @humorhealsus
To vote on new title names and freebies, visit us at humorhealsus.com for more information.

@humorhealsus   @humorhealsus